A Discipleship Guide for Lutherans

Volume 3

Authentic Relationships
Personal Transformation

Robert E. Logan
and Charles R. Ridley
with Dave Daubert

A **Discipleship Difference**

A DISCIPLESHIP GUIDE FOR LUTHERANS VOLUME 3 AUTHENTIC RELATIONSHIPS, PERSONAL TRANSFORMATION

By Robert E. Logan with Charles R. Ridley and Dave Daubert

Published by Logan Leadership
Visit us at www.loganleadership.com

ISBN-13: 978-1-944955-47-2
ISBN-10: 1-944955-47-X

Printed in the United States of America
2018- First Edition

24 23 22 21 20 19 18 17   10 9 8 7 6 5 4 3 2 1

Acknowledgement

We are grateful for the contribution of Pastor Dave Daubert, DMin, PhD in adapting this material originally created by Logan Leadership. Rev. Daubert is a Lutheran Pastor at Zion Lutheran Church in Elgin, Illinois and serves as CEO of Day 8 Strategies. He can be contacted at DDaubert@Day8Strategies.com.

Contents

Foreword to the Lutheran Discipleship Guides

By Dave Daubert, DMin, PhD

For many years I have worked with Lutheran congregations in the area of congregational renewal. I have done it from the inside as a parish pastor and from the outside as a consultant and denominational executive. Currently, I am doing both. I consult with congregations and I am a pastor in a congregation.

One thing that I have seen over and over again in this work is the need for increased emphasis on personal commitment as followers of Jesus. We Lutherans have an incredibly rich theological base. We have a wide reach across North America and around the world. We have one of the largest systems of colleges, universities and seminaries in the church world. But we have been better at producing church members than we have at producing committed followers of Jesus. Discipleship has not been our strongest feature.

In recent years, even that ability to produce committed church members has been tested. Like many Christian traditions in the United States, Lutherans are declining in numbers. This is true whether you are in the Lutheran Church — Missouri Synod or the Evangelical Lutheran Church in America. We are not unique in this — we have much company as religious participation is down across almost all Christian traditions.

At the same time, the news is not all gloom and doom. In both the ELCA and LC-MS there are many vibrant, sustainable and growing Lutheran congregations. While they may not make up the majority of our local churches, because of the numbers of Lutheran congregations in North America, their numbers are in the thousands. Yes, some of these congregations are simply doing the same old things and it still works in their contexts. Some of these places may be in trouble in the next decades.

But some of these congregations are simply doing good work. They are changing lives and engaging people in ministry. They are helping people become more engaged as disciples — followers of Jesus. In today's environment, that is essential.

Most people are busy. They don't need more busyness. But people are also running from thing to thing and often feeling rudderless in the sea of life. They may not want more activity but they are hungry for direction, meaning and purpose. They are longing for spiritual depth in a life that often feels shallow. And they are hoping that if they take something new up that it will actually be transformational and make a difference.

The Lutheran message could not be more helpful in a world like this. Lutherans understand that Christian faith starts with God. In his struggles, Martin Luther discovered that there is no way to God. All those brochures telling you how to get to God are distractions. There is no way to God. God in Christ comes to us. This is the heart of the incarnational message. Lutherans also know that when Christ comes to you, he comes with grace and peace. God is gracious and there are no strings attached. These basics mean that we simply receive Christ in faith and it is pure gift. No work involved!

But Lutherans have often stopped there. The grace that is ours has been our strongest message and, indeed, it is the most important and foundational message there is. Many other Christian traditions include or add our human work and effort to the equation. But not Lutherans. Grace is grace. Grace is free. There is nothing we can or need to add to it for grace to bring us life.

However, Lutheran theology believes deeply that such grace is transformational. People who believe are not the same as people who don't. A faithful life is lived out actively. It is grounded in love of the God who first loved us. It is directed toward our neighbors and the call to make the world look more like God desires. In other words, the Christian faith is both a free gift and a life-changing calling.

Before you open the first booklet, remember that Christ has come to declare to you that you are loved by God. That love is costly — it took Jesus to the cross. That love is persistent — the risen Christ comes back to each of us with the words, "Peace be with you." Simply believing this will change you.

With that foundation, this series of booklets should be a really helpful way to begin to focus on discipleship. The series approaches a wide variety of discipleship issues. It encourages people who trust that God loves them to take that love and put it to work doing things that further the agenda of a loving God. We are joined to Christ in our baptisms. We are to continue his work as the body of Christ. That means we not only know something. We DO something!

It may be that your congregation has a pattern for small groups and conversations already. If so, these may fit nicely into that. Many Lutheran congregations have mid-week services during Lent. Each of these booklets is five sessions and fits nicely in the five Wednesdays between Ash Wednesday and Holy Week. So you may want to pick one and use it with the congregation as a Lenten theme.

On the other hand, you may be starting from scratch. If so, get a friend to do this with you. The chance to have someone to discuss your thoughts with and to know someone is walking with you and you with them can keep you on course.

With many blessings as you use these guides in your journey of discipleship,

The Rev. Dave Daubert

Overview of the Tree of Discipleship

We don't have to be perfect to be Jesus' disciple, but we do have to know what we are signing up for and be willing to bring all areas of our lives to God. As Jesus discipled people, he expected that their discipleship would touch all aspects of their life, relationships, and even society as a whole.

A real disciple needs to embrace and be growing in all the dimensions of discipleship. We can't be ¾ of a disciple, picking and choosing, for a disciple when fully trained is like their teacher: Jesus (Luke 6:40). True discipleship is holistic: we can't be content to be growing in some areas and lacking in other areas.

As we've considered the nature of discipleship, we've created a diagram to represent the 8 dimensions of a disciple. As Jesus became incarnate and lived among us, these are the ways we see him living. Take a look at the diagram and categories that follow. Then evaluate your own life. Allow others to speak into your life as well: we never travel alone on the journey of allowing God to work in our lives.

Here are the eight dimensions of a disciple of Jesus:

- **Experiencing God**
- **Spiritual Responsiveness**
- **Sacrificial Service**
- **Generous Living**
- **Disciplemaking**
- **Personal Transformation**
- **Authentic Relationships**
- **Community Transformation**

Experiencing God: Intentionally and consistently engaging with God in deeper relationship

Supporting Scriptures:

> He answered, "Love the Lord your God with all your heart, and with all your soul, and with all your strength, and with all your mind; and your neighbor as yourself."
>
> — Luke 10:27

Behavioral Expressions:

- Increasing your awareness of God's love and presence
- Growing in the knowledge and grace of God
- Reflecting on and applying scripture in your everyday life
- Dialoguing authentically with God
- Worshiping God in spirit and in truth

Spiritual Responsiveness: Listening to the Holy Spirit and acting on what you hear

Supporting Scriptures:

> If we live by the Spirit, let us also be guided by the Spirit. — Galatians 5:25
>
> Trust in the Lord with all your heart, and do not rely on your own insight. In all your ways acknowledge him, and he will make straight your paths. — Proverbs 3:5-6
>
> But be doers of the word, and not merely hearers who deceive themselves. — James 1:22

Behavioral Expressions:

- Receiving guidance and empowerment from the Holy Spirit
- Discerning opportunities for involvement in God's work
- Checking what you're hearing with scripture and your faith community
- Acting in faith through loving obedience
- Listening for God's calling in your life

Sacrificial Service: Doing good works even when it's costly, inconvenient or challenging

Supporting Scriptures:

> *For we are what he has made us, created in Christ Jesus for good works, which God prepared beforehand to be our way of life. — Ephesians 2:10*

> *They asked only one thing, that we remember the poor, which was actually what I was eager to do. — Galatians 2:10*

Behavioral Expressions:

- **Blessing others with your words and deeds**
- **Partnering with others to minister in practical ways**
- **Ministering personally and appropriately to the poor**
- **Speaking up for people experiencing injustice**
- **Cultivating a compassionate heart**

Generous Living: Faithfully stewarding what God has given you for the advancement of God's Reign

Supporting Scriptures:

> *"For it is as if a man, going on a journey, summoned his slaves and entrusted his property to them; to one he gave five talents, to another two, to another one, to each according to his ability. Then he went away."— Matthew 25:14-15*

> *"Whoever is faithful in a very little is faithful also in much; and whoever is dishonest in a very little is dishonest also in much." — Luke 16:10*

Behavioral Expressions:

- **Managing your time and resources for kingdom purposes**
- **Using your spiritual gifts to bless others**
- **Giving your money generously and wisely**
- **Showing hospitality without favoritism**
- **Living out your God-given calling**

Disciplemaking: Making more and better followers of Christ by living the Great Commission

Supporting Scriptures:

"Go therefore and make disciples of all nations, baptizing them in the name of the Father and of the Son and of the Holy Spirit, and teaching them to obey everything that I have commanded you. And remember, I am with you always, to the end of the age."— Matthew 28:19-20

Behavioral Expressions:

- **Engaging in spiritual conversations with those who are not yet disciples of Jesus**
- **Explaining the good news and the way of Jesus**
- **Establishing new believers in a discipleship process**
- **Connecting people with a faith community**
- **Helping new followers make more followers**

Personal Transformation: Changing your behaviors and attitudes because of your relationships with God and others

Supporting Scripture:

Do not be conformed to this world, but be transformed by the renewing of your minds, so that you may discern what is the will of God—what is good and acceptable and perfect. — Romans 12:2

Behavioral Expressions:

- **Actively engaging with God in the examination of your heart**
- **Participating with God's healing work in your life**
- **Processing feedback and input from others**
- **Living out new priorities and changed behavior**
- **Increasingly bearing the fruit of the Spirit**

Authentic Relationships: Engaging with other people in ways that reflect the heart of God toward them

Supporting Scripture:

> *"In everything do to others as you would have them do to you; for this is the law and the prophets." — Matthew 7:12*

Behavioral Expressions:

- **Showing respect for all people**
- **Forgiving others and asking forgiveness**
- **Confronting each other with humility when necessary**
- **Praying with and for others**
- **Supporting each other honestly through life challenges**

Community Transformation: Personal involvement with others to facilitate positive change where you live and beyond

Supporting Scripture:

> *And the one who was seated on the throne said, "See, I am making all things new. —Revelation 21:5a*

> *Now to him who by the power at work within us is able to accomplish abundantly far more than all we can ask or imagine, to him be glory in the church and in Christ Jesus to all generations, forever and ever. Amen. — Ephesians 3:20-21*

Behavioral Expressions:

- **Participating in a faith community that reaches outside of itself**
- **Praying for healing and reconciliation in society**
- **Involving yourself in social justice needs in the broader community**
- **Caring for God's creation in practical ways**
- **Helping others create healthy lives and relationships**

How to use this guide

The eight topics just described flow from our previous book, The Discipleship Difference: Making Disciples while Growing as Disciples. The book lays out our full philosophy of making disciples. This is essentially an expansion of chapter two, where we discuss the qualities of a disciple.

- **What is a disciple?**

- **How would you know if you saw one?**

- **What behaviors would he or she exhibit?**

You can use these guides in a variety of ways to grow in holistic discipleship. Meet together in small groups, or better yet, groups of three or four. However you choose to go through them, go at your own pace: you can do one a week or one a month, whatever pace works best for you. The end result will be transformation — not of ourselves only — but of others and the whole of the community around us.

A Discipleship Guide for Lutherans has been developed to offer you an opportunity to encourage disciples new and old to Love God, Love Others, and Make Disciples.

Blessings,

Bob Logan

Authentic Relationships

Engaging with other people in ways that reflect the heart of God toward them

"In everything do to others as you would have them do to you; for this is the law and the prophets." — Matthew 7:12

Growing in Authentic Relationships

Authentic Relationships is one of eight discipleship guides for the Dimensions of Discipleship series. This edition has been specially written to help Lutheran Christians who are serious about deepening their discipleship commitments.

Dietrich Bonhoeffer believed that, "Christianity without discipleship is always Christianity without Christ." Concerned about what he termed "cheap grace," he believed that discipleship is an essential dimension for renewing the church in today's world.

Just as Luther believed that faith in Christ invited us into a relationship with Christ as a mentor, he also believed that faith in Christ called us to authentic relationships with our neighbors. In fact, Luther said, "it is necessary..." that we do the same thing, develop loving and meaningful relationships with others around us just as Christ had come to develop a loving and meaningful relationship with us.

These eight guides are organized according to the tree diagram above; examine it to see how all of the pieces fit together. It doesn't matter which guide you start with—start wherever you'd like and move on to wherever God is leading you next. When we live in the dynamic rhythm and flow of a missional life, we need to take our cues from the Holy Spirit.

The following five-part journey covers these five essential expressions of Authentic Relationships:

- **Showing respect for all people**

- **Forgiving others and asking forgiveness**

- **Confronting each other with humility when necessary**

- **Praying with and for others**

- **Supporting each other honestly through life challenges**

Meet together with a group of three or four others to talk through each of these expressions. Wait for and listen to responses from the heart. Encourage, challenge, and affirm one another. Go at your own pace: you can do one a week or one a month, whatever pace works best for you. Be sure to allow enough time to live into these behaviors.

I. Showing respect for all people

Key question: *How are you showing respect for all people? How can you grow in that?*

We treat people with respect because they are created in the image of God. Every single human being on the earth—from the poor living on the streets to kings and rulers, young and old, healthy and sick, people we like and people we don't. We are all created in the image of God and deserving of basic respect.

In addition, Luther understood that God can and does use anybody to make the world work. People are valuable because God actually works through them. This is one of the wonders of the world — that God orders the world to function by inviting and using people to help care for it and sustain it. People matter to God. Therefore people matter to us!

> "You can safely assume you've created God in your own image when it turns out that God hates all the same people you do."
>
> **— Anne Lamott, *Traveling Mercies***

How does that respect show? In many, many different ways, depending on the needs and on the relationship you have with the person: treating others with kindness, being honest, doing no harm, respecting the opinions of others even when you disagree, practicing generosity, taking time, showing patience.

The list of possibilities is as long as scripture itself.

Prayer and journaling

Who do you have the most trouble respecting? You can think of individuals or groups of people. (Consider economic status, race, culture, education, religion, sexual orientation, status, life choices, etc.) What is it that gets in the way of respect? What steps can you take to address that? As a first step, set aside half an hour to pray for people you have a tough time respecting. Journal about that experience afterwards.

This week read and reflect daily on the following scripture. Open a natural flow of conversational prayer with the Holy Spirit as you meditate on the scriptures, inviting the Spirit to connect with you. Then gather with those who journey alongside you and interact over the discipleship questions.

Genesis 1:26-27

Then God said, "Let us make humankind in our image, according to our likeness; and let them have dominion over the fish of the sea, and over the birds of the air, and over the cattle, and over all the wild animals of the earth, and over every creeping thing that creeps upon the earth." 27 So God created humankind in his image, in the image of God he created them; male and female he created them.

Genesis 33:10-11

Jacob said, "No, please; if I find favor with you, then accept my present from my hand; for truly to see your face is like seeing the face of God—since you have received me with such favor. 11 Please accept my gift that is brought to you, because God has dealt graciously with me, and because I have everything I want." So he urged him, and he took it.

James 2:1-13

My brothers and sisters, do you with your acts of favoritism really believe in our glorious Lord Jesus Christ? 2 For if a person with gold rings and in fine clothes comes into your assembly, and if a poor person in dirty clothes also comes in,

3 and if you take notice of the one wearing the fine clothes and say, "Have a seat here, please," while to the one who is poor you say, "Stand there," or, "Sit at my feet,"

4 have you not made distinctions among yourselves, and become judges with evil thoughts? 5 Listen, my beloved brothers and sisters. Has not God chosen the poor in the world to be rich in faith and to be heirs of the kingdom that he has promised to those who love him? 6 But you have dishonored the poor. Is it not the rich who oppress you? Is it not they who drag you into court? 7 Is it not they who blaspheme the excellent name that was invoked over you?

8 You do well if you really fulfill the royal law according to the scripture, "You shall love your neighbor as yourself." 9 But if you show partiality, you commit sin and are convicted by the law as transgressors. 10 For whoever keeps the whole law but fails in one point has become accountable for all of it. 11 For the one who said, "You shall not commit adultery," also said, "You shall not murder." Now if you do not commit adultery but if you murder, you have become a transgressor of the law. 12 So speak and so act as those who are to be judged by the law of liberty. 13 For judgment will be without mercy to anyone who has shown no mercy; mercy triumphs over judgment.

Discipleship questions

- When have you seen God in someone else? What has that looked like?

- Where do you see the image of God in those who do not yet follow Jesus?

- How can you more intentionally seek to see the image of God in people?

- Who do you know right now who needs to believe that the image of God resides in them?

- What are ways you show respect? What are ways you indicate it when you do not respect people?

- **Under what circumstances do you feel you must agree with a person in order to accept them?**

- **When have you felt unaccepted, like you don't belong?**

Action step questions

- **In light of our discussion, what is God asking you to do?**

- **How will you do this?**

- **When will you do this?**

- **Who will help you?**

- **With whom will you share what you have learned before we meet again?**

II. Forgiving others and asking forgiveness

Key question: Who do you need to forgive? Who do you need to ask for forgiveness?

Lutheranism was borne out of the deep sense of guilt that Luther experienced in his life. Struggling to be free of this, he had tried everything in the church's practices at that time but to no avail. Luther's struggle was grounded in a fear of a God who seemed angry and displeased with humanity. It was only when he rediscovered how deeply God loved him that he was able to begin to heal of the wounds that plagued him.

Today people are often less afraid of God's anger than they were 500 years ago. But part of living in the real world means we do sin against one another and are sinned against. Sometimes it's unintentional, sometimes it's intentional, but either way it hurts. What then? We have a hard time letting go of offenses against us. We have a hard time acknowledging the harm we've done to others. The forgiveness that lies at the heart of the gospel is the only thing that has the power to free us to live authentically within imperfect relationships with imperfect people.

This forgiveness isn't cheap. It doesn't mean we pretend no real harm was done. It doesn't mean we pretend to forget. It means we remember, acknowledge the hurt, and choose to let go anyway. Only through the power of God can we access this kind of forgiveness: we forgive because God forgave us (Col. 3:13).

> "A Christian fellowship lives and exists by the intercession of its members for one another, or it collapses. I can no longer condemn or hate a brother for whom I pray, no matter how much trouble he causes me."
>
> **— Dietrich Bonhoeffer**

Remember that both parts of the forgiveness process are essential: we need to ask for forgiveness from others and we need to offer forgiveness to others. One without the other is incomplete. When we confess our sins, do what we can to make it right, and embrace the fact that we are forgiven... then are we truly free to forgive others and not hold onto grievances. If we can't forgive others, we've likely not accepted God's forgiveness for ourselves.

This week read and reflect daily on the following scripture. Open a natural flow of conversational prayer with the Holy Spirit as you meditate on the scriptures, inviting the Spirit to connect with you. Then gather with those who journey alongside you and interact over the discipleship questions.

Luke 15:11-32

> *Then Jesus said, "There was a man who had two sons. 12 The younger of them said to his father, 'Father, give me the share of the property that will belong to me.' So he divided his property between them. 13 A few days later the younger son gathered all he had and traveled to a distant country, and there he squandered his property in dissolute living. 14 When he had spent everything, a severe famine took place throughout that country, and he began to be in need. 15 So he went and hired himself out to one of the citizens of that country, who sent him to his fields to feed the pigs. 16 He would gladly have filled himself with the pods that the pigs were eating; and no one gave him anything. 17 But when he came to himself he said, 'How many of my father's hired hands have bread enough and to spare, but here I am dying of hunger! 18 I will get up and go to my father, and I will say to him, "Father, I have sinned against heaven and before you; 19 I am no longer worthy to be called your son; treat me like one of your hired hands."' 20 So he set off and went to his father. But while he was still far off, his father saw him and was filled with compassion; he ran and put his arms around him and kissed him. 21 Then the son said to him, 'Father, I have sinned against heaven and before you; I am no longer worthy to be called your son.' 22 But the father said to his slaves, 'Quickly, bring out a robe—the best one—and put it on him; put a ring on his finger and sandals on his feet. 23 And get the fatted calf and kill it, and let us eat and celebrate; 24 for this son of mine was dead and is alive again; he was lost and is found!' And they began to celebrate. 25 "Now his elder son was in the field; and when he came and approached the house, he heard music and dancing. 26 He called one of the slaves and asked what was going on. 27 He replied, 'Your brother has come, and your father has killed the fatted calf, because he has got him back safe and sound.' 28 Then he became angry and refused to go in. His father came out and began to plead with him. 29 But he answered his father, 'Listen! For all these years I have been working like a slave for you, and I have never disobeyed your command; yet you have never given me even a young goat so that I might celebrate with my friends. 30 But when this son of yours came back, who has devoured your property with prostitutes, you killed the fatted calf for him!'*

31 Then the father said to him, 'Son, you are always with me, and all that is mine is yours. 32 But we had to celebrate and rejoice, because this brother of yours was dead and has come to life; he was lost and has been found.'"

Matthew 6:14-15

"For if you forgive others their trespasses, your heavenly Father will also forgive you; 15 but if you do not forgive others, neither will your Father forgive your trespasses."

Discipleship questions:

- **When is the last time you asked for forgiveness?**

- **When is the last time you asked for help with something you couldn't do on your own?**

- **What does it usually take to bring you to the point of asking for forgiveness? For help?**

- **What emotions surround that process?**

- **What response do you expect from others? What leads you to expect that response?**

"Doesn't that promise make you want to go and call that family member, that friend from whom you have felt alienated, with whom you have had harsh words, and share the good news, 'God forgives you. I forgive you,' and then ask forgiveness?"

— Mark Hanson

Action steps:

- **In light of our discussion, what is God asking you to do?**

- **How will you do this?**

- **When will you do this?**

- **Who will help you?**

- **With whom will you share what you have learned before we meet again?**

Forgiveness inventory

Write down wrongs you've done and wrongs that have been done to you on scraps of paper. Then, one by one, throw those scraps of paper into a bonfire.

III. Confronting each other with humility when necessary

Key question: *How are you being honest with those around you and confronting when necessary?*

God desires that we look honestly at ourselves and at where we fall short. For a faith that places such emphasis on repentance, this should not be so difficult for Christians, but it invariably is. We will sometimes go to great lengths to avoid looking at ourselves in the mirror.

For that reason, we need one another. Confronting others is not an enviable job, as any prophet can attest. But it is a necessary one. Sometimes God uses other people to point out where we are failing and how we need to change. For this reason, we need to be willing to confront one another honestly when it is necessary, even if it means we risk others being angry with us.

> "Forgiveness is the duct tape of Christian faith — and it works! Forgiveness binds together what would otherwise completely fall apart or stop functioning. It may not be the most stunning solution, but it's miraculous still."
>
> **— Mary C. Lind**

At the same time, we need to act and speak from a place of humility. We are no better than others, even when we need to point out a fault. Let us avoid the trap of the Pharisees.

This week read and reflect daily on the following scripture. Open a natural flow of conversational prayer with the Holy Spirit as you meditate on the scriptures, inviting the Spirit to connect with you. Then gather with those who journey alongside you and interact over the discipleship questions.

2 Samuel 12:1-13

And the LORD sent Nathan to David. He came to him, and said to him, "There were two men in a certain city, the one rich and the other poor. 2 The rich man had very many flocks and herds; 3 but the poor man had nothing but one little ewe lamb, which he had bought. He brought it up, and it grew up with him and with his children; it used to eat of his meager fare, and drink from his cup, and lie in his bosom, and it was like a daughter to him. 4 Now there came a traveler to the rich man, and he was loath to take one of his own flock or herd to prepare for the wayfarer who had come to him, but he took the poor man's lamb, and prepared that for the guest who had come to him." 5 Then David's anger was greatly kindled against the man. He said to Nathan, "As the LORD lives, the man who has done this deserves to die; 6 he shall restore the lamb fourfold, because he did this thing, and because he had no pity."7 Nathan said to David, "You are the man! Thus says the LORD, the God of Israel: I anointed you king over Israel, and I rescued you from the hand of Saul; 8 I gave you your master's house, and your master's wives into your bosom, and gave you the house of Israel and of Judah; and if that had been too little, I would have added as much more. 9 Why have you despised the word of the LORD, to do what is evil in his sight? You have struck down Uriah the Hittite with the sword, and have taken his wife to be your wife, and have killed him with the sword of the Ammonites.10 Now therefore the sword shall never depart from your house, for you have despised me, and have taken the wife of Uriah the Hittite to be your wife. 11 Thus says the LORD: I will raise up trouble against you from within your own house; and I will take your wives before your eyes, and give them to your neighbor, and he shall lie with your wives in the sight of this very sun. 12 For you did it secretly; but I will do this thing before all Israel, and before the sun." 13 David said to Nathan, "I have sinned against the LORD." Nathan said to David, "Now the LORD has put away your sin; you shall not die."

Galatians 2:11-14

But when Cephas came to Antioch, I opposed him to his face, because he stood self-condemned; 12 for until certain people came from James, he used to eat with the Gentiles. But after they came, he drew back and kept himself separate for fear of the circumcision faction. 13 And the other Jews joined him in this hypocrisy, so that even Barnabas was led astray by their hypocrisy. 14 But when I saw that they were not acting consistently with the truth of the gospel, I said to Cephas before them all, "If you, though a Jew, live like a Gentile and not like a Jew, how can you compel the Gentiles to live like Jews?"

Discipleship questions:

- **When have you sensed the need to confront someone? What did you do? What was the result?**

- **When is a time someone confronted you? How did that feel? What can you learn from that experience about confronting others?**

- **Do you find it difficult or easy to confront someone? Explain.**

- **How do you go about examining your heart and motives before talking with someone? What might a good process look like?**

Easy or hard?

Some people find it easy to confront others. Some find it difficult. Generally speaking, those who find it difficult need to speak out more often. Those who find it easy need to speak out less often. Which camp do you fall into? What might you do to make the necessary changes in how you confront?

Action steps:

- **In light of our discussion, what is God asking you to do?**

- **How will you obey God's prompting?**

- **When will you do it?**

- **Who will help you?**

- **With whom will you share what you have learned before we meet again?**

IV. Praying for and with others

Key question: *How are you praying for and with others?*

Our relationships have been described as horizontal and vertical: our horizontal relationships with one another and our vertical relationship with God. The priesthood of all believers means that all of us are called to lives of prayer. We have a connection to God and to others and we bring those two relationships together. We pray for those we are in horizontal relationship with... bringing their needs and concerns before God. We pray with others to God... bringing them into our relationship with God.

The gift and the power of prayer create a relational intimacy that calls for nothing less than full authenticity—with both God and others. At the same time, our relationship with God is enriched by our relationships with others. And our relationships with others are enriched by our relationship with God.

> "As we journey together through the time God has given us, may God give us the grace of a welcoming heart and an overflowing love for the new neighbors God has given us."
>
> **— Elizabeth Eaton**

This week read and reflect daily on the following scripture. Open a natural flow of conversational prayer with the Holy Spirit as you meditate on the scriptures, inviting the Spirit to connect with you. Then gather with those who journey alongside you and interact over the discipleship questions.

Colossians 1:3-14

> *In our prayers for you we always thank God, the Father of our Lord Jesus Christ, 4 for we have heard of your faith in Christ Jesus and of the love that you have for all the saints, 5 because of the hope laid up for you in heaven. You have heard of this hope before in the word of the truth, the gospel 6 that has come to you. Just as it is bearing fruit and growing in the whole world, so it has been bearing fruit among yourselves from the day you heard it and truly comprehended the grace of God.*

7 This you learned from Epaphras, our beloved fellow servant. He is a faithful minister of Christ on your behalf, 8 and he has made known to us your love in the Spirit.

9 For this reason, since the day we heard it, we have not ceased praying for you and asking that you may be filled with the knowledge of God's will in all spiritual wisdom and understanding, 10 so that you may lead lives worthy of the Lord, fully pleasing to him, as you bear fruit in every good work and as you grow in the knowledge of God. 11 May you be made strong with all the strength that comes from his glorious power, and may you be prepared to endure everything with patience, while joyfully 12 giving thanks to the Father, who has enabled you to share in the inheritance of the saints in the light. 13 He has rescued us from the power of darkness and transferred us into the kingdom of his beloved Son, 14 in whom we have redemption, the forgiveness of sins.

Praying the Lord's prayer

One way to structure our prayers so we're praying in alignment with the teachings of Jesus is to pray through the Lord's prayer. It's not the only pattern for prayer, but it is a good one.

Matthew 6:9-13

> *Pray then in this way:*
>
> *Our Father in heaven,*
>
> *hallowed be your name.*
>
> *(Prayer of recognition of who God is)*
>
> *10 Your kingdom come.*
>
> *(Prayer of hope for the future)*
>
> *Your will be done,*
>
> *on earth as it is in heaven.*

(Prayer of alignment with God's will)

11 Give us this day our daily bread.

(Prayer for the provision of needs)

12 And forgive us our debts,

as we also have forgiven our debtors.

(Prayer for forgiveness)

13 And do not bring us to the time of trial,

but rescue us from the evil one.

(Prayer for protection against temptation)

Discipleship questions:

- **Who or what do you feel compelled to pray for regularly?**

- **How often do you pray corporately with others? In what settings?**

- **What time do you have set-aside to pray individually?**

- **What settings are most conducive to prayer for you?**

- **What are some creative ways you can branch out in your prayers?**

 Prayer exercise

Pray in some different places and at different times than you normally do this week. If you usually pray in the morning, try praying at night. If you usually pray alone in silence, pray as you walk or run around the neighborhood. What other changes do you notice when you pray in different places and at different times?

Action steps:

- **In light of our discussion, what is God asking you to do?**

- **How will you do this?**

- **When will you do this?**

- **Who will help you?**

- **With whom will you share what you have learned before we meet again?**

V. Supporting each other honestly through life challenges

Key question: *How are you supporting others honestly through life challenges?*

People facing challenges are all around us. Being generous relationally is one of the most significant contributions we can make. As we relationally invest in others, we—as well as they— are transformed.

How does God invest in us? In a very personal, relational way Jesus came down as one of us, invested in long-term relationships, and willingly died on the cross. God the Father saw to the most intimate details of our creation, making us who God wanted us to be. The Holy Spirit lives within us, providing constant divine communication and direction. All of that required a lot more investment than writing a check and saying, "Be warm and well-fed." God has both warmed and fed us by standing with us through all things.

In the same way, we are to invest in other people to the degree that we are able. God placed the people who are in our lives there for a reason. We are to love them and reflect God to them. We are there to meet their needs. Yes, we only have so much relational capacity. We can only know so many people on a personal level. How are we investing the relational capacity we do have? The degree to which we do that reflects a life of generosity. The Lutheran understanding of Baptism uniting us with Christ means we live with and bear the presence of Christ at all times. We are Christ-bearers for the people around us and therefore continue the work of Jesus.

> "I will therefore give of myself as a Christ to my neighbor, just as Christ has offered himself for me."
>
> — **Martin Luther,** *The Freedom of a Christian*

This week read and reflect daily on the following scripture. Open a natural flow of conversational prayer with the Holy Spirit as you meditate on the scriptures, inviting the Spirit to connect with you. Then gather with those who journey alongside you and interact over the discipleship questions.

1 Thessalonians 2:8-13

So deeply do we care for you that we are determined to share with you not only the gospel of God but also our own selves, because you have become very dear to us. 9 You remember our labor and toil, brothers and sisters; we worked night and day, so that we might not burden any of you while we proclaimed to you the gospel of God. 10 You are witnesses, and God also, how pure, upright, and blameless our conduct was toward you believers. 11 As you know, we dealt with each one of you like a father with his children, 12 urging and encouraging you and pleading that you lead a life worthy of God, who calls you into his own kingdom and glory.

13 We also constantly give thanks to God for this, that when you received the word of God that you heard from us, you accepted it not as a human word but as what it really is, God's word, which is also at work in you believers.

John 15:9-17

As the Father has loved me, so I have loved you; abide in my love. 10 If you keep my commandments, you will abide in my love, just as I have kept my Father's commandments and abide in his love. 11 I have said these things to you so that my joy may be in you, and that your joy may be complete. 12 "This is my commandment, that you love one another as I have loved you. 13 No one has greater love than this, to lay down one's life for one's friends. 14 You are my friends if you do what I command you. 15 I do not call you servants any longer, because the servant does not know what the master is doing; but I have called you friends, because I have made known to you everything that I have heard from my Father.16 You did not choose me but I chose you. And I appointed you to go and bear fruit, fruit that will last, so that the Father will give you whatever you ask him in my name. 17 I am giving you these commands so that you may love one another.

"It is because God is the creator that a new creation is possible, and it is because of this new creation that the Christian life in time is possible."

— **George W. Forrell**

Discipleship questions:

- **With whom are you in regular relationship?**

- **How would you describe those relationships? Do you tend to be giving more or receiving more?**

- **What are some ways you could give to those you are in relationship with?**

- **What expectations do you have of others that make it difficult for you to invest in them?**

- **What are some of the ways people have invested in you over the course of your life?**

- **What impact did that have? What are some of the ways God has invested in you?**

Exercise

What do you already know God wants you to do? Search the scriptures for commands. Write down as many as you can.

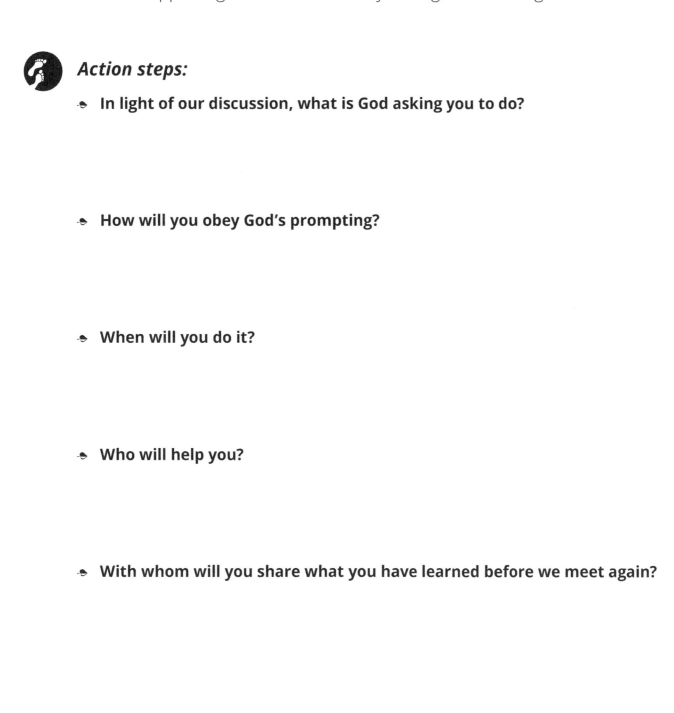

Action steps:

- **In light of our discussion, what is God asking you to do?**

- **How will you obey God's prompting?**

- **When will you do it?**

- **Who will help you?**

- **With whom will you share what you have learned before we meet again?**

Personal Transformation

Changing your behaviors and attitudes because of your relationships with God and others

Do not be conformed to this world, but be transformed by the renewing of your minds, so that you may discern what is the will of God—what is good and acceptable and perfect. — Romans 12:2

Growing in Personal Transformation

Personal Transformation is one of eight discipleship guides for the Dimensions of Discipleship series. This edition has been specially written to help Lutheran Christians who are serious about deepening their discipleship commitments.

Dietrich Bonhoeffer believed that, "Christianity without discipleship is always Christianity without Christ." Concerned about what he termed "cheap grace," he believed that discipleship is an essential dimension for renewing the church in today's world.

Personal transformation for Lutherans is about the process of faithful living over the long haul. Each day we when we awake we are challenged by Luther to remember our baptism. It is a daily promise that the failings of the previous day are forgiven and the call of the coming day lies ahead. Each day is both a clean slate and an opportunity for the new and abundant life that Jesus offers.

These eight guides are organized according to the tree diagram above; examine it to see how all of the pieces fit together. It doesn't matter which guide you start with—start wherever you'd like and move on to wherever God is leading you next. When we live in the dynamic rhythm and flow of a missional life, we need to take our cues from the Holy Spirit.

The following five-part journey covers these five essential expressions of Personal Transformation:

- **Actively engaging with God in the examination of your heart**

- **Participating with God's healing work in your life**

- **Processing feedback and input from others**

- **Living out new priorities and changed behavior**

- **Increasingly bearing the fruit of the Spirit**

Meet together with a group of three or four others to talk through each of these expressions. Wait for and listen to responses from the heart. Encourage, challenge, and affirm one another. Go at your own pace: you can do one a week or one a month, whatever pace works best for you. Be sure to allow enough time to live into these behaviors.

I. Actively engaging with God in the examination of your heart

Key question: *When and how are you setting aside time to reflect on your heart?*

Without taking the time to reflect on ourselves and our experiences, we can be exposed to great teachings and be a part of amazing experiences, yet not be transformed in any deep or meaningful way on a personal level. When we hear scripture, we need to reflect on it. When we do ministry, we need to consider how it is going and what we could do differently. When we experience God, we need to consider how that can change and mature us.

> "The gospel is not an idea, for example, that God loves us, although that is true. The gospel is good news. It's the announcement that something good and absolutely decisive for the universe has happened. The Christian good news is simply: Jesus is risen! Jesus will have the last word."
>
> — **Walter Bouman,** *Death Bed Letter*

What are the ways we can actively engage with the God who has announced something amazing in the death and resurrection of Jesus? How can we live out our lives with more intentionality?

We can reflect in silence and prayer, listening for the voice of God and being open to the leading of the Holy Spirit. We can discuss and pray together with others in the body of Christ, asking for their insights and perspectives. We can work with a coach, mentor or spiritual director who asks us questions to help us discern where God might be at work in our lives. Engaging in this study with a few other people can be a great first step toward deeper reflection.

Journal

Take some time alone and write or draw about these three questions: What have I been hearing from God lately? What am I learning from my experiences? Who might be able to speak into my life right now? Don't worry about getting the words just right—you are the only one who will be reading it—just say what you want to say.

This week read and reflect daily on the following scripture. Open a natural flow of conversational prayer with the Holy Spirit as you meditate on the scriptures, inviting the Spirit to connect with you. Then gather with those who journey alongside you and interact over the discussion questions.

Colossians 3:1-17

So if you have been raised with Christ, seek the things that are above, where Christ is, seated at the right hand of God. 2 Set your minds on things that are above, not on things that are on earth, 3 for you have died, and your life is hidden with Christ in God. 4 When Christ who is your life is revealed, then you also will be revealed with him in glory.

5 Put to death, therefore, whatever in you is earthly: fornication, impurity, passion, evil desire, and greed (which is idolatry). 6 On account of these the wrath of God is coming on those who are disobedient. 7 These are the ways you also once followed, when you were living that life.

8 But now you must get rid of all such things—anger, wrath, malice, slander, and abusive language from your mouth. 9 Do not lie to one another, seeing that you have stripped off the old self with its practices 10 and have clothed yourselves with the new self, which is being renewed in knowledge according to the image of its creator. 11 In that renewal there is no longer Greek and Jew, circumcised and uncircumcised, barbarian, Scythian, slave and free; but Christ is all and in all!

12 As God's chosen ones, holy and beloved, clothe yourselves with compassion, kindness, humility, meekness, and patience. 13 Bear with one another and, if anyone has a complaint against another, forgive each other; just as the Lord has forgiven you, so you also must forgive.

14 Above all, clothe yourselves with love, which binds everything together in perfect harmony. 15 And let the peace of Christ rule in your hearts, to which indeed you were called in the one body. And be thankful. 16 Let the word of Christ dwell in you richly; teach and admonish one another in all wisdom; and with gratitude in your hearts sing psalms, hymns, and spiritual songs to God. 17 And whatever you do, in word or deed, do everything in the name of the Lord Jesus, giving thanks to God the Father through him.

James 1:22-25

But be doers of the word, and not merely hearers who deceive themselves. 23 For if any are hearers of the word and not doers, they are like those who look at themselves in a mirror; 24 for they look at themselves and, on going away, immediately forget what they were like. 25 But those who look into the perfect law, the law of liberty, and persevere, being not hearers who forget but doers who act—they will be blessed in their doing.

Luke 18:9-14

He also told this parable to some who trusted in themselves that they were righteous and regarded others with contempt: 10 "Two men went up to the temple to pray, one a Pharisee and the other a tax collector. 11 The Pharisee, standing by himself, was praying thus, 'God, I thank you that I am not like other people: thieves, rogues, adulterers, or even like this tax collector. 12 I fast twice a week; I give a tenth of all my income.' 13 But the tax collector, standing far off, would not even look up to heaven, but was beating his breast and saying, 'God, be merciful to me, a sinner!' 14 I tell you, this man went down to his home justified rather than the other; for all who exalt themselves will be humbled, but all who humble themselves will be exalted."

Discipleship questions

- Describe a time when you intentionally set aside some time for reflection. How did you do that? What came of it?

- What are your impressions of the story of the tax collector and the Pharisee?

- When is a time when you really felt God speaking to you? How did God do that?

- What strategies have been most helpful in getting you to reflect? Which others might you want to try?

- What gets in the way of your reflecting? What steps might you take to overcome that barrier?

Action step questions

- In light of our discussion, what is God asking you to do?

- How will you do this?

- When will you do this?

- Who will help you?

- With whom will you share what you have learned before we meet again?

II. Participating with God's healing work in your life

Key question: *How are you participating with God's healing work in your life?*

God desires to do healing work in your life. It's not as if some people need healing and others don't. We all need healing in different ways, whether physical, emotional, relational, spiritual, or some other type of healing. We live in a broken world and we are broken people. We stand in need of God's gracious healing, with nothing to offer to God in return.

Yet with healing comes risk. We often need to step forward and be willing to be healed. Not everyone who needs healing is willing to be healed. To recognize oneself in need of healing and to open oneself to the Spirit in order to do God's work takes a great deal of courage and trust. It is not easy and it is often not passive.

> "This life therefore is not righteousness, but growth in righteousness, not health, but healing, not being but becoming, not rest but exercise. We are not yet what we shall be, but we are growing toward it, the process is not yet finished, but it is going on. This is not the end but it is the road."
>
> **—Martin Luther**

We need to stand before God with empty hands and allow God to provide for healing in our lives. That might mean we need to forgive, to let go, to stay, to accept. We do not know what God may ask of us when we put ourselves in God's hands. What we do know is that God desires us to become our best selves, reflections of the image of God, healed and whole.

Journal

In what ways do you need healing? Meditate on the broken areas in your life and consider what healing might look like. What would you need to let go of in order for God to heal that area of your life?

This week read and reflect daily on the following scripture. Open a natural flow of conversational prayer with the Holy Spirit as you meditate on the scriptures, inviting the Spirit to connect with you. Then gather with those who journey alongside you and interact over the discussion questions.

John 5:1-9

After this there was a festival of the Jews, and Jesus went up to Jerusalem. 2 Now in Jerusalem by the Sheep Gate there is a pool, called in Hebrew Beth-zatha, which has five porticoes. 3 In these lay many invalids—blind, lame, and paralyzed. 5 One man was there who had been ill for thirty-eight years. 6 When Jesus saw him lying there and knew that he had been there a long time, he said to him, "Do you want to be made well?" 7 The sick man answered him, "Sir, I have no one to put me into the pool when the water is stirred up; and while I am making my way, someone else steps down ahead of me." 8 Jesus said to him, "Stand up, take your mat and walk." 9 At once the man was made well, and he took up his mat and began to walk. Now that day was a sabbath.

Matthew 4:23-24

Jesus went throughout Galilee, teaching in their synagogues and proclaiming the good news of the kingdom and curing every disease and every sickness among the people. 24 So his fame spread throughout all Syria, and they brought to him all the sick, those who were afflicted with various diseases and pains, demoniacs, epileptics, and paralytics, and he cured them.

Matthew 9:10-13

And as he sat at dinner in the house, many tax collectors and sinners came and were sitting with him and his disciples. 11 When the Pharisees saw this, they said to his disciples, "Why does your teacher eat with tax collectors and sinners?" 12 But when he heard this, he said, "Those who are well have no need of a physician, but those who are sick. 13 Go and learn what this means, 'I desire mercy, not sacrifice.' For I have come to call not the righteous but sinners."

James 5:16

Therefore confess your sins to one another, and pray for one another, so that you may be healed. The prayer of the righteous is powerful and effective.

1 Peter 2:24-25

He himself bore our sins in his body on the cross, so that, free from sins, we might live for righteousness; by his wounds you have been healed. 25 For you were going astray like sheep, but now you have returned to the shepherd and guardian of your souls.

"Only people who are capable of loving strongly can also suffer great sorrow, but this same necessity of loving serves to counteract their grief and heals them."

— Leo Tolstoy

Discipleship questions:

- **What areas of your life stand in need of healing?**

- **Are you willing to be healed?**

- **What will that healing require of you?**

- **What fears do you have around being healed?**

- **How might God be able to use you if you cooperate with his healing work in your life?**

 **Action steps:**

- **In light of our discussion, what is God asking you to do?**

- **How will you do this?**

- **When will you do this?**

- **Who will help you?**

- **With whom will you share what you have learned before we meet again?**

III. Processing feedback and input from others

Key question: *How are you requesting and processing constructive input from others?*

How do we know if we're doing well? In certain fields such as math, there is a clearly right answer and clearly wrong answers. In other fields, such as spirituality, relationships, and personal transformation, it's not quite so clear. There are different perspectives to take into account and different goals that may—or may not—be agreed upon. It would be great if we had some built-in way to determine how we're doing, but that's not the way it works. Like many other things, God has set this up organically in such a way that we need each other.

> "Anyone who is to find Christ must first find the church. How could anyone know where Christ is and what faith in him is unless he knew where his believers are?"
>
> **— Martin Luther**

We need to find ways to open ourselves up to constructive input from others. Sometimes people, both inside and outside the church, will give us unsolicited feedback. In those cases, we need to evaluate the feedback to see if it is constructive and helpful. If so, we need to reflect on it and find ways to incorporate it into our lives. If not, we are free to discard it. Yet most of the time people will not give uninvited feedback. We need to ask for it. We can often find a great deal of useful feedback simply by asking people we trust who are in a position to give helpful feedback.

This week read and reflect daily on the following scripture. Open a natural flow of conversational prayer with the Holy Spirit as you meditate on the scriptures, inviting the Spirit to connect with you. Then gather with those who journey alongside you and interact over the discussion questions.

Ecclesiastes 4:9-13

> *Two are better than one, because they have a good reward for their toil.10 For if they fall, one will lift up the other; but woe to one who is alone and falls and does not have another to help. 11 Again, if two lie together, they keep warm; but how can one keep warm alone?*

12 And though one might prevail against another, two will withstand one. A threefold cord is not quickly broken.

13 Better is a poor but wise youth than an old but foolish king, who will no longer take advice.

Galatians 2:11-14

But when Cephas came to Antioch, I opposed him to his face, because he stood self-condemned; 12 for until certain people came from James, he used to eat with the Gentiles. But after they came, he drew back and kept himself separate for fear of the circumcision faction. 13 And the other Jews joined him in this hypocrisy, so that even Barnabas was led astray by their hypocrisy. 14 But when I saw that they were not acting consistently with the truth of the gospel, I said to Cephas before them all, "If you, though a Jew, live like a Gentile and not like a Jew, how can you compel the Gentiles to live like Jews?"

Proverbs

The righteous gives good advice to friends,

but the way of the wicked leads astray. (12:26)

By insolence the heedless make strife,

but wisdom is with those who take advice. (13:10)

Without counsel, plans go wrong,

but with many advisers they succeed. (15:22)

A word fitly spoken

is like apples of gold in a setting of silver. (25:11)

Discipleship questions:

- Who has given you unsolicited feedback that was constructive and helpful? What did you do with that feedback?

- Who have you asked for feedback lately? Who might be in a good position to give it?

- How can you tell the difference between constructive and destructive feedback?

- What makes it difficult for you to ask for and receive feedback? What steps might you take to address those roadblocks?

Action steps:

- **In light of our discussion, what is God asking you to do?**

- **How will you obey God's prompting?**

- **When will you do it?**

- **Who will help you?**

- **With whom will you share what you have learned before we meet again?**

IV. Living out new priorities and changed behavior

Key question: *How are you living out new priorities and changed behavior?*

The whole point of the gospel isn't to get us to think different things or even to do different things... it's to help us become different. Through God's active presence, God shapes each of us more and more into the unique person we were meant to be. We are transformed by our encounter with God, and that transformation shows itself in new priorities and new actions. We live out the change that God has worked within us.

> "God comes straight out with it: 'I am the Lord your God.' This is the decision: God has decided to be your God. For God wants to be as close to you as your next breath, to be the one who gives you confidence and value, to open a future to you and the freedom of the Word. God wants to be the one to whom you turn for whatever you need."
>
> **— James Nestingen**

This week read and reflect daily on the following scripture. Open a natural flow of conversational prayer with the Holy Spirit as you meditate on the scriptures, inviting the Spirit to connect with you. Then gather with those who journey alongside you and interact over the discussion questions.

Acts 9:1-22

> *Meanwhile Saul, still breathing threats and murder against the disciples of the Lord, went to the high priest 2 and asked him for letters to the synagogues at Damascus, so that if he found any who belonged to the Way, men or women, he might bring them bound to Jerusalem. 3 Now as he was going along and approaching Damascus, suddenly a light from heaven flashed around him. 4 He fell to the ground and heard a voice saying to him, "Saul, Saul, why do you persecute me?" 5 He asked, "Who are you, Lord?" The reply came, "I am Jesus, whom you are persecuting. 6 But get up and enter the city, and you will be told what you are to do." 7 The men who were traveling with him stood speechless because they heard the voice but saw no one.*

8 Saul got up from the ground, and though his eyes were open, he could see nothing; so they led him by the hand and brought him into Damascus. 9 For three days he was without sight, and neither ate nor drank.

10 Now there was a disciple in Damascus named Ananias. The Lord said to him in a vision, "Ananias." He answered, "Here I am, Lord." 11 The Lord said to him, "Get up and go to the street called Straight, and at the house of Judas look for a man of Tarsus named Saul. At this moment he is praying, 12 and he has seen in a vision a man named Ananias come in and lay his hands on him so that he might regain his sight." 13 But Ananias answered, "Lord, I have heard from many about this man, how much evil he has done to your saints in Jerusalem; 14 and here he has authority from the chief priests to bind all who invoke your name." 15 But the Lord said to him, "Go, for he is an instrument whom I have chosen to bring my name before Gentiles and kings and before the people of Israel; 16 I myself will show him how much he must suffer for the sake of my name." 17 So Ananias went and entered the house. He laid his hands on Saul and said, "Brother Saul, the Lord Jesus, who appeared to you on your way here, has sent me so that you may regain your sight and be filled with the Holy Spirit." 18 And immediately something like scales fell from his eyes, and his sight was restored. Then he got up and was baptized, 19 and after taking some food, he regained his strength. For several days he was with the disciples in Damascus, 20 and immediately he began to proclaim Jesus in the synagogues, saying, "He is the Son of God." 21 All who heard him were amazed and said, "Is not this the man who made havoc in Jerusalem among those who invoked this name? And has he not come here for the purpose of bringing them bound before the chief priests?" 22 Saul became increasingly more powerful and confounded the Jews who lived in Damascus by proving that Jesus was the Messiah.

Mark 5:1-20

They came to the other side of the sea, to the country of the Gerasenes. 2 And when he had stepped out of the boat, immediately a man out of the tombs with an unclean spirit met him. 3 He lived among the tombs; and no one could restrain him any more, even with a chain; 4 for he had often been restrained with shackles and chains, but the chains he wrenched apart, and the shackles he broke in pieces; and no one had the strength to subdue him. 5 Night and day among the tombs and on the mountains he was always howling and bruising himself with stones. 6 When he saw Jesus from a distance, he ran and bowed down before him; 7 and he shouted at the top of his voice, "What have you to do with me, Jesus, Son of the Most High God? I adjure you by God, do not torment me."

8 For he had said to him, "Come out of the man, you unclean spirit!" 9 Then Jesus asked him, "What is your name?" He replied, "My name is Legion; for we are many." 10 He begged him earnestly not to send them out of the country. 11 Now there on the hillside a great herd of swine was feeding; 12 and the unclean spirits begged him, "Send us into the swine; let us enter them." 13 So he gave them permission. And the unclean spirits came out and entered the swine; and the herd, numbering about two thousand, rushed down the steep bank into the sea, and were drowned in the sea.

14 The swineherds ran off and told it in the city and in the country. Then people came to see what it was that had happened. 15 They came to Jesus and saw the demoniac sitting there, clothed and in his right mind, the very man who had had the legion; and they were afraid. 16 Those who had seen what had happened to the demoniac and to the swine reported it. 17 Then they began to beg Jesus to leave their neighborhood. 18 As he was getting into the boat, the man who had been possessed by demons begged him that he might be with him. 19 But Jesus refused, and said to him, "Go home to your friends, and tell them how much the Lord has done for you, and what mercy he has shown you." 20 And he went away and began to proclaim in the Decapolis how much Jesus had done for him; and everyone was amazed.

"We stand at a crossroads. Either we must become more radical about the gospel or we would be better off to forget it altogether."

– Gerhard Forde, *Radical Lutheranism*

Discipleship questions:

- **Describe a time in your life that you successfully changed a behavior or habit. What was it that enabled you to make that change?**

.

- **What motivates you?**

- **When have you had a true encounter with God? How did that change you?**

- **How would you like others to describe you? What needs to change in your life for that to be an accurate description?**

Exercise

Make a list of what you see as your priorities, and write each one on a separate sticky note. Make a list of the ways in which you spend your time, and write each one on a separate sticky note. Now put the notes in two columns on the wall or a whiteboard. How do items in the two lists align? Where do you see connections? What do you need to do more of in order to make your time reflect your priorities? What do you need to do less of?

Action steps:

- **In light of our discussion, what is God asking you to do?**

- **How will you do this?**

- **When will you do this?**

- **Who will help you?**

- **With whom will you share what you have learned before we meet again?**

V. Increasingly bearing the fruit of the Spirit

Key question: *How are you growing in the fruits of the Spirit?*

As we are transformed, we should increasingly see evidence of the fruits of the Spirit in our lives. Where do we see love? Joy? Peace? What actions of ours can we point to that demonstrate patience? Kindness? Goodness? What evidence can we find of faithfulness? Gentleness? Self-control? The more we can see specific instances of these qualities in our lives, the more we know that the Spirit is truly doing its transformative work in our lives... because these qualities are the result of that work.

Christian Schwarz, in his book *The 3 Colors of Love*, makes the case that there is only one fruit of the Spirit—Love—along with its 8 descriptors: joy, peace, patience, kindness, goodness, faithfulness, gentleness, and self-control. When you compare 1 Corinthians 13 and Galatians 5, you'll see there's a great deal of correlation. Whether you see the fruits of the Spirit as 9 or 1, the issue is that we need to grow. We need to assess where we're at and how to deepen character. Stagnation is not a viable option.

> "The gospel of Christ converts us, but it also nourishes us. We need to keep receiving Christ over and over again."
>
> **– Gene Veith, *The Spirituality of the Cross***

This week read and reflect daily on the following scripture. Open a natural flow of conversational prayer with the Holy Spirit as you meditate on the scriptures, inviting the Spirit to connect with you. Then gather with those who journey alongside you and interact over the discussion questions.

Galatians 5:13-26

> *For you were called to freedom, brothers and sisters; only do not use your freedom as an opportunity for self-indulgence, but through love become slaves to one another. 14 For the whole law is summed up in a single commandment, "You shall love your neighbor as yourself." 15 If, however, you bite and devour one another, take care that you are not consumed by one another. 16 Live by the Spirit, I say, and do not gratify the desires of the flesh.*

17 For what the flesh desires is opposed to the Spirit, and what the Spirit desires is opposed to the flesh; for these are opposed to each other, to prevent you from doing what you want. 18 But if you are led by the Spirit, you are not subject to the law. 19 Now the works of the flesh are obvious: fornication, impurity, licentiousness, 20 idolatry, sorcery, enmities, strife, jealousy, anger, quarrels, dissensions, factions, 21 envy, drunkenness, carousing, and things like these. I am warning you, as I warned you before: those who do such things will not inherit the kingdom of God. 22 By contrast, the fruit of the Spirit is love, joy, peace, patience, kindness, generosity, faithfulness, 23 gentleness, and self-control. There is no law against such things. 24 And those who belong to Christ Jesus have crucified the flesh with its passions and desires. 25 If we live by the Spirit, let us also be guided by the Spirit. 26 Let us not become conceited, competing against one another, envying one another.

I Corinthians 13:4-7

Love is patient; love is kind; love is not envious or boastful or arrogant 5 or rude. It does not insist on its own way; it is not irritable or resentful; 6 it does not rejoice in wrongdoing, but rejoices in the truth. 7 It bears all things, believes all things, hopes all things, endures all things.

Discipleship questions:

- If someone invisible were to follow you around for a week, observing your behavior, what qualities do you think they might use to describe you?

- What character qualities do you consider your strengths? What character qualities do you consider your weaknesses?

- How have you approached improving your weaknesses?

- What are your thoughts on Christian Schwarz's interpretation of the fruit of the Spirit (described above)? How might that perspective assist you in your growth?

- What practices might help you increasingly bear the fruit of the Spirit?

Action steps:

- **In light of our discussion, what is God asking you to do?**

- **How will you obey God's prompting?**

- **When will you do it?**

- **Who will help you?**

- **With whom will you share what you have learned before we meet again?**

Journal the fruit of the Spirit

Dedicate one page to each of the nine fruits of the Spirit. Underneath each, write as many examples as you can of times you experienced each of those qualities... either by demonstrating them yourself or by receiving them from others.

What's Next?

So you've completed this guide. What now? Is there another dimension of discipleship you need to zoom in on? If so, which one?

Because the various sections of *A Discipleship Guide for Lutherans* aren't meant to be used in any particular order, it's up to you to do some listening to the Holy Spirit. Take a look at the big picture and decide where God is leading you next. With a holistic system, it's always a surprise. No matter which guide you choose next, you're engaged in an ongoing action-reflection process as you continue living incarnationally. Each section in the series is listed below:

Experiencing God: Intentionally and consistently engaging with God in deeper relationship

Spiritual Responsiveness: Listening to the Holy Spirit and acting on what you hear

Sacrificial Service: Doing good works even when it's costly, inconvenient or challenging

Generous Living: Faithfully stewarding what God has given you for the advancement of God's Reign

Disciplemaking: Making more and better followers of Christ by living the Great Commission

Personal Transformation: Changing your behaviors and attitudes because of your relationships with God and others

Authentic Relationships: Engaging with other people in ways that reflect the heart of God toward them

Community Transformation: Personal involvement with others to facilitate positive change where you live and beyond

About the Printed Guide Volumes

The full series of *A Discipleship Guide for Lutherans* has been gathered into a four-volume printed set. Here is how the sections are presented in the printed volumes.

Volume 1

Experiencing God: Intentionally and consistently engaging with God in deeper relationship

Supporting Scriptures:

> He answered, "Love the Lord your God with all your heart, and with all your soul, and with all your strength, and with all your mind; and your neighbor as yourself."
> — Luke 10:27

Behavioral Expressions:

- **Increasing your awareness of God's love and presence**
- **Growing in the knowledge and grace of God**
- **Reflecting on and applying scripture in your everyday life**
- **Dialoguing authentically with God**
- **Worshiping God in spirit and in truth**

Spiritual Responsiveness: Listening to the Holy Spirit and acting on what you hear

Supporting Scriptures:

> If we live by the Spirit, let us also be guided by the Spirit. — Galatians 5:25

> Trust in the Lord with all your heart, and do not rely on your own insight. In all your ways acknowledge him, and he will make straight your paths. — Proverbs 3:5-6

> But be doers of the word, and not merely hearers who deceive themselves. — James 1:22

Behavioral Expressions:

- **Receiving guidance and empowerment from the Holy Spirit**
- **Discerning opportunities for involvement in God's work**
- **Checking what you're hearing with scripture and your faith community**
- **Acting in faith through loving obedience**
- **Listening for God's calling in your life**

Volume 2

Sacrificial Service: Doing good works even when it's costly, inconvenient or challenging

Supporting Scriptures:

For we are what he has made us, created in Christ Jesus for good works, which God prepared beforehand to be our way of life. — Ephesians 2:10

They asked only one thing, that we remember the poor, which was actually what I was eager to do. — Galatians 2:10

Behavioral Expressions:

- **Blessing others with your words and deeds**
- **Partnering with others to minister in practical ways**
- **Ministering personally and appropriately to the poor**
- **Speaking up for people experiencing injustice**
- **Cultivating a compassionate heart**

Generous Living: Faithfully stewarding what God has given you for the advancement of God's Reign

Supporting Scriptures:

"For it is as if a man, going on a journey, summoned his slaves and entrusted his property to them; to one he gave five talents, to another two, to another one, to each according to his ability. Then he went away." — Matthew 25:14-15

"Whoever is faithful in a very little is faithful also in much; and whoever is dishonest in a very little is dishonest also in much." — Luke 16:10

Behavioral Expressions:

- **Managing your time and resources for kingdom purposes**
- **Using your spiritual gifts to bless others**
- **Giving your money generously and wisely**
- **Showing hospitality without favoritism**
- **Living out your God-given calling**

Volume 3

Authentic Relationships: Engaging with other people in ways that reflect the heart of God toward them

Supporting Scripture:

> *"In everything do to others as you would have them do to you; for this is the law and the prophets." — Matthew 7:12*

Behavioral Expressions:

- **Showing respect for all people**
- **Forgiving others and asking forgiveness**
- **Confronting each other with humility when necessary**
- **Praying with and for others**
- **Supporting each other honestly through life challenges**

Personal Transformation: Changing your behaviors and attitudes because of your relationships with God and others

Supporting Scripture:

> *Do not be conformed to this world, but be transformed by the renewing of your minds, so that you may discern what is the will of God—what is good and acceptable and perfect. — Romans 12:2*

Behavioral Expressions:

- **Actively engaging with God in the examination of your heart**
- **Participating with God's healing work in your life**
- **Processing feedback and input from others**
- **Living out new priorities and changed behavior**
- **Increasingly bearing the fruit of the Spirit**

Volume 4

Disciplemaking: Making more and better followers of Christ by living the Great Commission

Supporting Scriptures:

"Go therefore and make disciples of all nations, baptizing them in the name of the Father and of the Son and of the Holy Spirit, and teaching them to obey everything that I have commanded you. And remember, I am with you always, to the end of the age."— Matthew 28:19-20

Behavioral Expressions:

- **Engaging in spiritual conversations with those who are not yet disciples of Jesus**
- **Explaining the good news and the way of Jesus**
- **Establishing new believers in a discipleship process**
- **Connecting people with a faith community**
- **Helping new followers make more followers**

Community Transformation: Personal involvement with others to facilitate positive change where you live and beyond

Supporting Scripture:

And the one who was seated on the throne said, "See, I am making all things new. —Revelation 21:5a

Now to him who by the power at work within us is able to accomplish abundantly far more than all we can ask or imagine, to him be glory in the church and in Christ Jesus to all generations, forever and ever. Amen. — Ephesians 3:20-21

Behavioral Expressions:

- **Participating in a faith community that reaches outside of itself**
- **Praying for healing and reconciliation in society**
- **Involving yourself in social justice needs in the broader community**
- **Caring for God's creation in practical ways**
- **Helping others create healthy lives and relationships**

About the Authors

Dr. Robert E. Logan has over 40 years of ministry experience, including church planting, pastoring, consulting, coaching, and speaking. Having seen a great deal, Bob remains on the cutting edge of ministry through hands-on missional involvement. Bob earned his DMin from Fuller Theological Seminary. He counts it a privilege to walk alongside ministry leaders and help catalyze their ministries toward fulfilling the call God has placed on them, and he thrives in developing holistic and transformative resources that can easily be implemented in any context. Bob enjoys cycling and volunteering in a recovery community.

Dr. Charles R. Ridley has utilized his expertise in the area of measurement and assessment in the development of the church planter profile, which has shaped the foundation of church-planter selection all over the world. He has also done extensive work on coach competencies and assessments, conducting a qualitative international research project. A licensed psychologist and professor at Texas A&M University, Chuck earned his PhD in counseling psychology from the University of Minnesota.

About Logan Leadership

Our vision is every person living, growing and multiplying together as disciples of Jesus who demonstrate the Kingdom of God among all peoples.

Our mission is catalyzing leaders to accelerate their movement toward this vision.

Our approach integrates biblical principles with social science insights by helping leaders...

- **sharpen thinking skills**
- **focus actions**
- **contextualize solutions**
- **create reproducible processes**
- **increase ministry capacity**

Find out more about us at **http://loganleadership.com**.

Appendix

Love God | Love Others | Make Disciples

Logan Leadership is the central hub for information and resources to assist you in your personal growth and your ministry. With decades of experience coaching and consulting with leaders worldwide, our desire is to equip leaders to live, grow, and multiply together as disciples of Jesus who demonstrate the Kingdom of God among all peoples.

We're all about helping you get where you want to go. That looks different for each ministry or organization. Depending on your goals, we can provide targeted coaching, training, resource development, assessment, and/or consulting.

Over the years, we've helped hundreds of churches, denominations and mission organizations meet and exceed their goals. That can mean implementing discipleship processes, retooling leadership development, turning around congregations in decline, or any number of other aims.

Coaching — The accountability and clarity that coaching provides gives you the follow through you need to accomplish the goals you've set for yourself and your ministry.

Consulting — We can enter your ministry situation to help you find contextualized solutions for your specific needs.

Training — We design interactive training systems geared toward coaches, church planters, disciplers, pastors and key leaders.

Resource Development — We can create and/or adapt Logan Leadership resources that speak effectively and appropriately to the culture and people of your organization.

Assessments — Using God's Word and proven social science insights, we offer a number of effective assessment tools that help you and your organization make smart decisions.

Find out more at **https://loganleadership.com**.

Discipleship Resources

To fulfill the Great Commission, we must be faithful to make disciples of Jesus. Logan Leadership has created several resources to assist you in your personal discipleship journey and in encouraging others toward a closer walk with God.

Discipleship for Episcopalians is available in a downloadable PDF format as well as in print. Visit the Discipleship Guides Shop on our website to learn more and to purchase your copy at **https://loganleadership.com/G4D**.

The Discipleship Difference

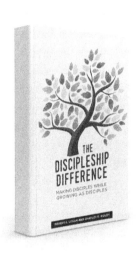

Every person is different and we all reflect God in different ways. So why is our typical approach to discipleship the same across the board? The Discipleship Difference lays out an intentional, holistic, and relational approach to discipleship that is individualized to meet each person wherever they are.

The Discipleship Difference is available in print and Kindle at **http://amazon.com** or at **https://loganleadership.com/DD**. Contact us for bulk discount.

Discipleship Cohort

How many years have you been trying to get discipleship going in your context? Are you willing to try something different? The Discipleship Cohort is a year-long cohort for implementing discipleship in your ministry context. Offered only once per year, this group is a deep dive into the eight dimensions of discipleship outlined in the companion book for this course, The Discipleship Difference.

Check **https://loganleadership.com/DC** for details on the next open application period.

Disciple Assessment

Your church will only grow as well as the disciples that you develop. How can you reliably measure discipleship progress? The portrait of Jesus in the four gospels serves as our guide. Disciples seek to live and love like Jesus. The Disciple Assessment provides a snapshot of where you are in 8 dimensions of a disciple of Jesus, and is appropriate for individuals, small groups, churches, and missional communities. Learn more at **http://discipleassessment.com**.

Training Opportunities

As a ministry leader, you know how difficult it can be to gather a group together for training. What if you could gather together virtually to walk through training together?

Logan Leadership offers an online training specifically for pastors and ministry leaders who want to train others via Sublimeety, a subscription- based web platform that establishes flexible processes to facilitate more efficient and productive virtual meetings and trainings. This training material is highly  interactive and offers special resources and practical exercises to sharpen your team's group leadership skills. We give you the tools, and you add your unique perspective to personalize the experience for your leaders. Want to learn more?
Visit us at: **http://go-sublime.com**.